A Church Wedding
YOUR SPECIAL DAY

Ewen Gilchrist

A LION POCKETBOOK
Oxford · Batavia · Sydney

Text copyright © 1992 Ewen Gilchrist
This edition copyright © 1992 Lion Publishing
Illustrations copyright © 1992 Pat Gregory

Published by
Lion Publishing plc
Sandy Lane West, Oxford, England
ISBN 0 7459 1649 X
Albatross Books Pty Ltd
PO Box 320, Sutherland, NSW 2232, Australia
ISBN 0 7324 0491 6

First edition 1992

A catalogue record of this book is available
from the British Library.

Printed and bound in Malta

Contents

1	Congratulations!	4
2	Love Is a Mirror	8
3	Once Upon a Dream	10
4	Countdown Checklist	22
5	Who Calls the Tune?	26
6	In-laws, Outlaws	28
7	That's Your Job	30
8	Successful Sex	32
9	Making Ends Meet	36
10	Cheating	39
11	Till Death Us Do Part	43

1

Congratulations!

So it's true. You and the person who has become so special in your life have decided to get married. The day when you wondered if he would ever speak to you, if she would ever smile at you, are now a fond memory. You are now so certain that you love each other and want to stay together that you're ready to make promises that will last a lifetime.

For reasons which are real to you but hard to explain in words, you may feel that it's very important to get married in church. People often talk about the church in terms of 'hatch, match and despatch'. They find their way to church or chapel for the big events—baptism, marriage and funeral. Right now you're in the 'match' category, with the hope of 'hatch' in the future (possibly, maybe) and 'despatch' a long time away!

To be honest, a lot of people planning a wedding will not have seriously involved themselves with a

church for years. You may be wondering if it is acceptable for a couple to consider getting married in church when they have no real connection with that church. Or is it perhaps hypocritical to have a Christian wedding when the couple are not quite sure exactly what a Christian is?

Your approaching marriage may be the opportunity to find out. So lay aside any prejudices or presumptions you may have. Lay aside those half-baked images that so many of us cart around in our heads about Christians and the church. Maybe you've been amazed over the months and years to discover that your partner could love a creep like you—the creep you know you sometimes are. Maybe you'll be amazed to discover that God knows you even better than your future partner does—and he still offers you friendship and love, trust and understanding.

☆ *When should we meet the minister?* If you do want a church wedding, the sensible thing to do is to

5

speak to your local minister right at the start. For one thing, you'll want to book a date that suits all concerned. Believe it or not, clerics are busy people, and their weddings diaries can be booked up months in advance.

☆ *Will we get a welcome?* You may be worrying that the minister will frown on you if you are not a church member or perhaps disapprove of your lifestyle. It is true that some churches will not marry couples where one or both partners have been previously married, but others do allow remarriage. And some churches will offer a blessing on a civil wedding, if they cannot perform the wedding themselves. But again, the best way to find out is to contact your local minister. Many times, you'll be surprised and pleased by the welcome you receive.

☆ *Will we have to attend pre-marriage classes?* Some churches do run classes for couples who wish to get married. Couples may join a class with other couples or have private sessions with the minister. They all have the same aim: to help couples get the best possible start in married life. They also have the bonus effect of helping you to get to know the minister better. That way, come the big day, the minister is not marrying strangers and you aren't being married by someone you hardly know.

☆ *Will we be preached at?* Ministers will also want to share with you something of the Christian faith.

After all, if you are to be married in a church, it's only natural that some expression of the Christian faith should be present in the wedding service. Ministers may well want to talk with you privately about the love which brings you together as future husband and wife; and about the love of God which Christians believe is at the heart of all good things. They may well try to explain to you that the source of the love which brings you to the point of marriage is no less than God himself.

2

Love Is a Mirror

Someone once said that marriage is a mirror in which we see ourselves more clearly than ever before. Falling in love and preparing for marriage is an opportunity to look inwards, in a healthy sort of way, and discover more about ourselves.

You need to take time to discover who you really are, so that you can share yourself with your partner in marriage. What are your good points, the things you like about yourself? Our society encourages people to be suitably modest about their abilities and achievements—but sometimes this can backfire and prevent us from evaluating honestly what is really good in ourselves.

You also need to face up to your limitations and the things about yourself that you don't like. What can be changed? What can't be changed?

And, at a simpler level, you need to identify what your aims and goals are.

☆ *Are you looking for money, power, success, status?* You're going to need some of each, but how much?

☆ *What other priorities do you have?* Are you concerned to stay healthy? stay thin? get thin? have lots of friends? What matters most?

☆ *How do you like to spend your time?* Do you like to be alone, or enjoying a hobby, or out and about talking to others?

☆ *Are you interested in the needs of others?* Do you think it's important to serve and help people in different ways?

☆ *Do you care about things that might be described as spiritual or religious?* How will these values affect the way you organize your life or hope to raise your children?

And when you have discovered these things for yourself, you need to discuss them with your partner. You may not agree on all of them, at least not straight away. But you do need to talk through them all, to make sure that you can indeed walk through life together in harmony.

3

Once Upon a Dream

As you approach the time of your wedding, the actual details of the event loom large in your mind. Will you get the whole thing right? Will your family and friends enjoy it with you? Will it be an event you can look back on with pleasure?

First of all, think about what a wedding is for. It's a celebration! You're affirming your love, trust and faithfulness to your partner before family and friends. And you're giving them a party, perhaps as a thank-you for their love and support.

You're also telling society that you and your partner are a new family unit. This is quite different from simply living together, when family and community don't really know whether or not you are a family, and whether or not you'll be staying together. And without the security of marriage, living together isn't even a fair trial of marriage.

If you're marrying in church you may also be

saying something special about how you want God to be the foundation of your home and marriage. You're not just staging an event, the finale to a beautiful romance. You're affirming a new beginning—the start of the whole new two-people-become-one adventure, which is marriage as God intended. And so you are dedicating your marriage to God and asking for his help as you learn to grow together.

So what makes a proper wedding? Colour-coordinated bridesmaids? Colour-contrasted in-laws? Printed personalized napkins? Lacy garters? Endless alcohol? Pick up a wedding magazine for a totally up-to-date picture of how to dispose of any extra savings you might have. 'It's your day,' croon the advertisements. 'You deserve to treat yourself to the very best.'

Well, it is your day, and a very special one. But often the regalia-pushers are trying to manipulate you into assuming that spending vast amounts on yourselves and your guests is the only fit expression of your joy. To put it bluntly, weddings are big business for specialists in traditional wedding trappings, and the occasion can be as commercialized as Christmas.

Your wedding day is not meant to be a production-line affair. It should be unique, because you are unique as a couple, because your love for each other is wonderfully different from the love other couples share.

The most memorable weddings I've attended

stood out *not* because of the lavishness of the flowers, dress or food—although none of these things were neglected—but because the couple made the guests a very real part of the day. The bride and groom were more than mere showpieces. They somehow managed to make that special occasion express something of the spirit of their relationship and the joy they wanted to share. As a result, the guests felt relaxed and happy.

In some cases, this atmosphere of celebration has been enriched by different people making their own special contribution. Family and friends often enjoy using their talents as photographers, bakers, cake-decorators, flower arrangers (and growers), drivers or dressmakers to enhance the occasion.

And they do enhance it, often doing a better job than the professionals because they care enough to take the time and trouble to do things really well!

Of course, a do-it-yourself wedding is not intrinsically superior. One friend of mine worked long years before she became a bride, and her choice was to spend the money she had earned in buying just what she wanted. It gave her immense joy to provide herself and all her guests with a glorious treat. Personally paid for in her own name. And it was *fun!*

And what about all those rules of etiquette? Will the world shatter if the ushers don't wear carnations, if the groom's mother doesn't wear a hat, if the bride's Aunt Mary sits on the groom's side of the church? Not a bit. Neither will it come crashing down if the bride wears a coloured outfit at the service and makes a speech at the reception. The groom does not have to sit shaking in the vestry till the last moment. He can go to the church ahead of time to greet his guests, and he can even look confident and cheerful.

So create your own dream. Here is a brief guide to wedding conventions. Read, mark, and cheerfully adapt.

A Proper Wedding

CAST

Bride

Groom

Attendants (usually children and young women)

Best Man

Ushers (often three young men)

Bride's father, or similar escort

Minister

Bride's mother, and groom's parents

Friends and relatives of the bride and groom

★ Children can come to weddings, and behave, and enjoy themselves. Plan to include them. Make sure they are seated where they can *see* what goes on. And make sure there is some food at the reception that they will enjoy.

★ Do any of your guests have difficulty getting around? Check on access to the church and reception, and make any additional arrangements that will help your guests enjoy the day.

ACT 1, SCENE 1

A church, decorated with flowers. Music is playing softly. The ushers are at the door, greeting the relatives and friends as they arrive in the half hour before the time appointed for the wedding. They hand out service sheets or books. Friends and relatives of the bride sit on the left of the church, those of the groom on the right.

★ For some reason, one side always seems to have more guests. Many people today really won't mind where they sit.

The groom and his best man arrive. The best man keeps reaching into his pocket, to check that he still has the wedding rings.

The minister arrives. Then the bride's mother and the bride's attendants. The best man and groom stand at the front of the church. One of the ushers escorts the bride's mother to her seat at the front of the church. All the late-arriving guests hurry to their seats.

SCENE 2

The attendants and the minister wait for the bride and her father. They all form a procession, often the minister leading, then the bride holding her father's right arm, followed by her attendants. A secret sign is given. The music in the church ceases. Then a triumphant chord indicates the beginning of the procession music and the bridal party enters. All stand. The groom waits at the top of the aisle, supported as much as necessary by the best man!

At the front of the church, the characters stand in this order:

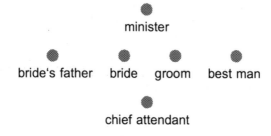

The minister welcomes all the guests, and the service begins. The bride hands her flowers to the chief attendant. Sometimes the bride's father gives his daughter's hand to the minister, who then hands it to the groom. The bride and groom exchange vows. The minister announces that rings will be given as a sign of the marriage. The best man still has them in his pocket. *Phew!* Hymns are sung. There is a reading. Prayers are said. The bride and groom go off somewhere to sign the register. Two other people sign as witnesses.

★ Ask your minister about the different forms of service that you can use. Choose the one that best reflects what you want to say.

★ Ask how many hymns you can have in the service. Take time to choose ones that reflect the joy of the occasion. 'The Lord's my Shepherd' is very moving—at funerals. Choose something else!

★ Ask if you can select your own reading. It may be a Bible passage or a passage that says something special to both of you.

★ Think about the prayers. How do you want God to be involved in your marriage? Do the prayers reflect this?

★ Will your aunt/sister/cousin be allowed to sing a solo/play the harp while you are signing the register? Where should they stand or sit for the best sound?

★ Who will provide the music for the hymns and the two processions? Can you choose the music?

★ Can photos be taken during the service? Check with the minister. Think, too—do you really *want* all that whirring and clicking?

SCENE 3

Another secret sign, another triumphant chord. The bride and groom walk down the aisle. They are husband and wife. The best man and chief attendant follow on. Then the other attendants. And the bride's father with the groom's mother, and the bride's mother with the groom's father, folding together in pairs like a pack of cards. Tears are shed.

★ After the service is often the point when photos are taken. It is therefore the time when many guests get a little bored. Plan what photos you want, and try to have them taken as quickly as possible. The occasion matters more than the pictures of it.

★ Some guests may find it tiring to stand and watch. Is there anywhere that older people can sit? Where children can play?

The bridal party lead the way to the reception, either walking or in cars. The guests follow, the best man and ushers making sure that everyone knows where to go and how to get there.

ACT 2, SCENE 1

Another room, also decorated with flowers. The bride's parents, and perhaps the groom's parents, and the bride and groom, are welcoming their guests. Some of the guests clutch presents. The best man is ready to put them in a safe place. Drinks may be served as the guests assemble for the meal.

The small attendants find some mud. No one else has found any. It is special small-attendant mud. Kind aunts cluck and fuss.

★ Don't panic if some little detail goes wrong. No one will mind. But if you start getting upset, your guests may feel uncomfortable. In a few years' time, that splosh on the smallest bridesmaid may well be the most endearing touch in the whole photo album.

★ What *do* you say to your guests in the receiving line? Well, don't hold everything up while you think. Welcome them cheerfully, and move them on. You can take time to walk round and talk to them later on.

At last everyone gathers for the meal. They eat. And chat. And revive some delightful family feuds which they have been saving for this day. Someone photographs them as they glower at each other and sends them the photos three weeks later, which duly shames them!

SCENE 2

The best man calls everyone to order. The bride and groom take their place behind a towering cake. Together they pick up a gleaming knife and make the first cut. Cheers and applause. Everyone knows how hard it is to get a knife through concrete. A helper races forward and whisks the cake away. They have pneumatic cutters in the kitchen.

As slices of cake are distributed and glasses are filled, the best man asks for silence. He gets giggles. The bride's father stands up. He reads a polite speech. An embarrassing little tale about his daughter when she was small. The bride lowers her eyelids and plans to sabotage his dahlias. It's over. The bride's father proposes a toast to the bride and groom.

All stand. 'The bride and groom.'

All sit. The groom stands. He thanks the bride's father. He thanks everyone he can think of, whether or not they are at the wedding. This is not his finest hour. He searches the room for fresh inspiration. The bridesmaids. He says he has never seen such pretty young women. 'Not even the bride,' booms some tactless uncle from the back.

All stand for a hasty toast to the bridesmaids.

★ A tip for speechmakers: speak loud enough so everyone can hear you, and keep it short!

★ The bride may make a speech.

The best man stands. He tries to tell funny tales about the groom. Even his best friends have to force their laughter. Hastily he moves on to read the greetings from people who have not been able to come to the wedding. They are curiously illegible. He should have pencilled in the hard words earlier. Oh well, never mind. A toast to, to, um, well . . . all the best to one and all.

★ This is not the time for risqué humour. Choose your best man with care.

SCENE 3

The bride and groom have disappeared. No one saw them go. No one saw a few other people slip out either. And here are the bride and groom—look at that HAT, see the BOW TIE—ready to go off on their honeymoon. Someone brings their car round.

See the balloons, the streamers, the tin cans. Hear the whoops of glee. The couple drive off into the sunset, hoping that it will be fully dark before anyone else sees them.

4

Countdown Checklist

How long does it take to plan a wedding? You may spend a year or more dreaming, devising and hand-crafting ribbon flowers. Or you can crack through the lot in about two months and still retain your sanity. To help you plan, here is a list of tasks to consider.

Even if you plan to have friends do some of these jobs, it is a good idea to get their agreement well in advance.

☆ Visit your minister to fix the date.

☆ Decide on your reception plans. A meal? A dance? A party?

☆ Decide with both sets of parents how many people to invite.

☆ Decide on your catering arrangements. Book the hotel or hall, if that is your choice, and outside caterers. Also book the band or disc jockey if you are planning a dance.

☆ Book your honeymoon. Check your passports if you plan to go abroad. Will you have a new name when you travel?

☆ Book the photographer.

☆ Order cars for the wedding party, if needed.

☆ Arrange for you and your partner to visit the doctor for a full health check and to discuss family planning. Check on any immunizations you may need for your honeymoon trip.

☆ Arrange to have the wedding cake made.

☆ Choose wedding outfits for the wedding party. Don't forget to select the right shoes for all concerned.

☆ Draw up a final guest list and prepare invitations. Send them out, ideally at least eight weeks before the event.

☆ Decide on how you will deal with questions about what gifts you would like. Make a gift list if you wish.

☆ Plan your wedding service. Choose hymns, readings, and music for your entrance, exit, and the time you are signing the registers. Discuss your choice with the organist or whoever is providing the music. If you wish, have service sheets printed.

☆ Arrange for a rehearsal.

☆ Select wedding rings. A ring for the groom is optional.

☆ Keep a list of acceptances and refusals to the invitations.

☆ Order flowers for the bride and bridesmaids; buttonholes for the groom, best man and ushers, and perhaps the groom's father; and more elaborate corsages for the bride's and the groom's mothers.

☆ Check on floral arrangements at the church and at the reception. Order flowers if necessary.

☆ Check the legalities. Make sure that you obtain any licences etc. that are required. Your minister

will tell you what is needed in your choice of church.

☆ If you are planning to change your name, notify your bank, doctor, dentist and others.

☆ Choose presents for the best man and bridesmaids. (These may be presented to them publicly on the day, or handed over quietly.)

☆ Select clothes for going away in and for the honeymoon.

☆ Arrange to have your hair cut about two weeks before the wedding. If necessary, arrange a hairdresser appointment on the day itself.

☆ Send out thank-yous for gifts as they arrive.

☆ Give the final numbers of guests to whoever is doing the catering.

☆ Take time for you and your partner to be by yourselves. More and more of your days are invaded by wedding this and wedding that. Sometimes this can be exciting, sometimes it's frightening. So make time to be together, without relatives, just to reassure yourselves that you mean everything to each other.

5

Who Calls the Tune?

The big day is over, the honeymoon a memory, the presents, tasteful and otherwise, have been unwrapped and acknowledged with thank-you notes. Marriage has begun. What happens now?

Now is the time when you really begin to work out your new relationship. It's not a question of gathering sufficient romance or wedding-day glamour at the beginning, in the hope that it will provide enough fuel to keep the fire of love burning. It's about letting the seedling relationship that you have grow bigger and stronger, and providing the atmosphere that will help it to flourish.

How will your partnership work out? What are the terms of the relationship that are described in the marriage vows? Does the bride promise to 'obey' her husband?

In the beginning, man and woman were created equal partners. It was only after they allowed sin and evil into the world that there had to be a rule that the man should be head over the wife. Some say that the ideal is to return to an equal relationship, to which both bring different talents. Others say that there has to be a leader.

Either approach can work. But Christian marriage puts both in a special light. It means first accepting Jesus and his teaching as the standard for your life, and then serving your partner.

Within a marriage, circumstances change. Children come (or do not come), parents grow old and die, mid-life arrives, and so on. Amidst all of this, every couple must learn how to communicate with each other and support each other. It is not that one partner develops the plan that will direct the marriage and the other fits in with it. Both must learn to share the tasks, to communicate with each other, to provide the initiative or provide support as needed.

'Who calls the tune?' is perhaps a bottom-line question, for those times when all else fails. When you simply cannot agree with each other on a particular issue, how on earth do you reach a decision? In a loving relationship, it should mean that each is prepared to accept the decision that is better for the other, so that both can agree on which course of action is best for their relationship as a whole.

6
In-laws, Outlaws

However you work out the leadership issue in your marriage, one thing is certain: you, as a couple, must decide what is right for your lives together. The Bible is quite clear when it says that a man must *leave* his parents to build a marriage with his wife, and it is true for the wife also. In-laws should not be allowed to invade a marriage. But they shouldn't be treated like dirt either.

In popular tale, mothers-in-law are a bad joke. *Her* mother can't believe he's good enough. *His* mother thinks she's selfish, flighty, and a rotten cook. Fathers-in-law are curiously absent, not daring to take on either side!

The truth is that both sets of parents want the best for their offspring, and they can't quite let go of the habit of checking that their baby is being treated just right. The in-law relationship can easily be seen as an unwelcome intrusion, something to be pushed away.

But there is a better way of handling things, so that the relationship is happy and rewarding on both sides.

☆ *Agree with your partner that your relationship is now number one.* You both have to leave your parents, physically and emotionally, to build a marriage.

☆ *Agree that you will both try to build a good relationship with both sets of parents.* Visit them, invite them over ... possibly, in a while, let them hold the baby ...

☆ *Agree that he will deal with his mum and dad, and she will deal with her mum and dad.* So *he* explains why you're spending this Christmas with her parents; *she* explains why you don't want extra help with the house, thanks very much, Dad. Remember, they'll forgive their own baby such harshness, but they may resent it in the newcomer.

☆ *Laugh.* Everyone says a few tactless things. Be ready to forgive, ready to say sorry, ready to try again.

7
That's Your Job

Marriage is full of rather jokey stereotypes: the hapless wife who can't change a fuse; the chunky, check-shirted husband who can fix everything; the supremely efficient wife who can cook, clean, decorate . . . *and* still look alluring at the end of the day; the bungling husband who is to home maintenance what Attila the Hun was to the Preservation of Historic Buildings.

We like our stereotypes. And although we recognize that people are often far removed from these images, nevertheless we do carry around in our head certain presumptions about what our partner will be and what our partner will do once wedded bliss has come upon us.

Much has changed in recent years. It may well be that the wife goes out to a paid job and the husband stays at home with the children. And he may turn out to be a better housekeeper than she could ever be; she may be a better wage earner. Or both may work from home. Or both may go out to a paid job. In finding out what suits you best as a couple, you stand a better chance of being happier in your role.

Marriage is about being committed to each other, not to the stereotyped roles which we may feel pressurized to conform to. So be honest about what your talents and preferences are, about the kind of role you want for yourself in your career and in your home. There is no 'standard' wife or 'standard' husband. The only true standard is the love you have for each other, and the freedom you give each other to let your God-given talents flourish.

8

Successful Sex

Freud made a living out of it. Comedians make a
laugh out of it. The Victorians made a monster out of
it. What? Sex!

You know sex! That primeval drive, that un-
controllable urge. That much sung of, much
dreamed of passion. That huge disappointment.
That thing that can bring two people such incredible
joy and delight and satisfaction. It's the same thing.
And it's one of the most powerful and beautiful
things that two people can share in marriage.

I'd like to introduce you to some different
approaches and attitudes to sex. You may have
something in common with more than one.

☆ *The Caveman Approach*. This sexual philosophy
   is alive and well in many places. Man wants
   woman, man lays woman, man is satisfied, man
   (probably) falls asleep. To the caveman, the

woman is a possession and sex is something he gets when he wants.

☆ *The Ballooning Approach.* Ah, the view of the world from a hot air balloon! There you are, floating gently and effortlessly across the clouds, gasping in awe and admiration at the scenic beauty and the thrill of it all.

Ecstasy and awe can also describe, truly, the experiences of husband and wife as they celebrate their love sexually. But getting to that delighted condition will not have been effortless. A lot of patience is needed, along with the ability to learn humbly from mistakes.

☆ *The Theoretical Approach.* This is where the would-be lover becomes the victim of twentieth-century sexual introspection. We now know all about those mischievous hormones; we understand the cunning complexities of the woman's monthly cycle; we are sensitive towards the power of libido (though we hope no one actually asks us what it means); we are well read on every form of family planning and we have analyzed, scrutinized and become mesmerized by the deep, soul-touching significance of love in contemporary music culture: 'Do it!'

But, by the time we're actually ready for action, the passion has gone, replaced by fun-destroying caution and confusion. Too much thinking can be bad for you!

☆ *The It's-A-Gift Approach.* This understanding of sex starts with the basic assumption that sex is simply a gift from God, purposefully intended to give great pleasure to two people in love.

The it's-a-gift approach accepts that sex is a physical need, as ordinary and as normal as any other need, even though life and happiness do not depend on it. It doesn't for a moment try to dismiss sex as an insignificant or tasteless dimension of marriage.

On the contrary, sex is there to explore, to share, to enjoy—providing a unique and, at times, wonderful way of saying 'I love you' to your partner. It can seal and enrich a marriage, as the couple become 'one flesh', to quote the Bible.

Sex is something to thank God for! And couples also need something of the patience and gentleness and forgiveness of God as they learn together how good sex can be.

9
Making Ends Meet

Ever since you started getting pocket money you probably noticed one startling fact about money: if you had more of it, you could buy more things. What you have—whatever the amount—still leaves something tantalizingly out of reach.

Getting married is a time when you have to re-evaluate your financial position to suit the new arrangement. There is the cost of the wedding to consider, unless parents are obligingly providing it all. There is the cost of setting up home together and of merging your finances. Meanwhile there are wedding magazines to tempt you with their dream of up-to-date homes, with complete sets of fine china, elegant cutlery and gorgeous wooden furniture . . . and the bedrooms . . .

Meanwhile, back in your oppressive little room, the main hurdle to overcome is simply making sure that your expenditure doesn't exceed your income.

Oh, there are wonderful ways of getting loans to make a little extra cash flow your way before you actually earn it, but the reality remains. And if you have two or more bank accounts and a bunch of credit cards, or even an impulsive taste for bargains, you can get overdrawn beyond what you can reasonably repay.

It's frighteningly easy to acquire habits that mean you are living beyond your income, buying things you really don't need to maintain the lifestyle of your contemporaries. Don't underestimate the pressure of seeing your friends' homes becoming increasingly streamlined. But recognize the temptation for what it is. And quite apart from these luxuries, bills for gas, electricity and telephone are painful certainties, while household repairs and car maintenance are just some of the more predictable of life's calamities.

As you enter marriage, you need to do some level-headed talking about your priorities in order to avoid major disagreements later about the way one or other of you uses the money. Here are some ideas to get you going.

☆ *Discuss your priorities for spending.* Do you want to save up—perhaps for a home, or a car, or a family? Do you want to spend freely, at least for the first few years of your married life? Is getting the maximum number of possessions important? Or do you want to set aside some money for giving to others?

☆ *Analyze your budget.* Discuss what your income is. Find out what you can reasonably expect to buy with it. Discuss how much you spend, looking at weekly, monthly and yearly expenses. Do you need to cut back on spending? Where can you do so? Do you need to set limits for spending—say, in the supermarket, when clothes shopping, or at Christmas? Are there ways you could spend less? Check that you are getting any grants or allowances to which you are entitled. Could you share equipment and skills with friends and neighbours? Do you need to earn more, and how could you do that?

☆ *Decide how you want to manage your finances.* Do you want to combine them, or keep them as separate as possible? Either approach can work. The important thing is to agree on what you do.

10
Cheating

The congregation is hushed. The bridal couple are but seconds away from becoming husband and wife. The minister's words are clear, familiar to all, even clichéd—but oh, so precious to those two people: 'to have and to hold from this day forward . . .'

Clammy hands, loving hands, trusting hands. 'I now declare you to be husband and wife.' Now the hands can part, because a greater union has somehow been created. Marriage. Is it just an institution or a deep, spiritual truth? Is it a legal technicality or a mysterious and powerful union? The fact is, the vast majority of couples, at the precise moment when they are declared married, are genuinely committed to each other, to the promises they have made, to their future together.

So what goes wrong? How come so many couples soon forget the promises and the dreams and the love, and become another divorce statistic?

Marriage is for ever—the good times and bad.

Sometimes it has to do with adultery. Even in our age when people talk glibly about sexual relationships, adultery is still something of a dirty word. It means a particular form of cheating and deceit, where one partner gives their body to someone else. Their intrusion into the marriage can only bring harm.

The bit in the Ten Commandments about not committing adultery often provokes sniggers. It is also used as false proof that being a Christian is not fun. Countless people the world over would sigh as they affirm that adultery brings more misery than anything else, hurting any number of people as trust and love crumble. It's not considered particularly prudish to stop at the sign that says *Danger—Edge of Cliff*. In the same way, it's only sensible to recognize that adultery can kill a marriage.

But there are other ways of cheating. Less spectacular, less titillating, less frowned upon, but in their way just as destructive. When all is said and done, adultery is when one partner takes the love and affection and energy and time which should be directed to their partner and gives it to someone, or *something*, else.

Perhaps your partner becomes so obsessed about 'getting on' in their work that it becomes a kind of lover. They come home late too often, days off are interrupted, holidays impossible to plan. And even when they're home, their body may be with you but their mind is still on the job. In its subtle, unwitting way, that is a kind of adultery. And it kills marriages.

There are professions that bring a high-risk factor to marriage. Those in which a lot of shift work is involved, where your partner can be away days or weeks on end, where long-awaited, much-needed days off and holidays can be scrapped at the last moment. It's wise to recognize these difficulties in advance and to try to consider ways of coping with those tensions. Otherwise the job, which is understandably precious, can become an adulterous affair.

For that matter, so can football or the aerobics class or any other hobby. When does one partner begin to lose out? When does the marriage begin to lose out because the other partner is cheating, not with a person but with a club, a group, an interest that seemed so innocent at first?

And there are yet more subtle ways of cheating, as far removed from sexual adultery as you could think.

It is possible to cheat on a marriage while doing something that is, in itself, very valuable. Such as taking time to help other people—voluntary work, perhaps. Or caring for an elderly parent. Or even taking care of the children. It is all too easy to get so caught up in taking care of other people that you neglect the most important human relationship in your life.

In marriage, your commitment is to each other, first and foremost, because you are meant to be more important to each other than anyone or anything else. For all kinds of reasons, sometimes that perspective can be lost. Take the time to set it right, to do things together, to be alone together.

11
Till Death Us Do Part

'Excuse me, the automatic switch-off on my new kettle is faulty; I'd like a refund.'

'I bought this sweater last week, and the stitching's given way in two places. I want you to replace it.'

'This is the third time this year that my video recorder's gone on the blink. I don't want you to repair it again; I want my money back.'

'I'm very disappointed in the performance of my new wife. She's not meeting expectations at all, especially in bed. I want to replace her.'

Hold it!

Consumer goods usually carry guarantees and money-back promises to protect the customer from faulty workmanship. Marriage carries a different

kind of promise, to protect the couple from making
hasty, harmful decisions when the going gets tough.

> *I take you*
> *to be my wife/husband,*
> *to have and to hold*
> *from this day forward;*
> *for better, for worse,*
> *for richer, for poorer,*
> *in sickness and in health . . .*
> *till death us do part.*

The marriage vows are the terms of commitment,
not the terms of a contract. Contracts can be ripped
up and thrown away when either party fails to keep
its side of the promise. 'You have not installed my
double-glazing by the date agreed; so I'm cancelling
the order. Good day!' Fair enough: business is
business, a contract is a contract.

But a marriage is something else. A marriage is an
opportunity for two people to show each other
something of the nature of love which God shows for
them.

God's love is not contractual: 'You've sinned.
You all broke the contract. I'm having nothing more
to do with you.' God's love for us is unconditional. It
is the love he shows us through Jesus. He came as
God's son to pay the penalty for our failings, and
endured great pain as he died, so that we could enjoy
a restored relationship with God, if we only accept
it. God has made that agreement with us—a special
covenant.

And on your wedding day, the promises that you make are a reminder that something of that covenant love should be seen in your marriage. No strings attached, no small type, no catches—you are promising to love your partner through thick and thin, and to respond to the love that is offered to you. And to survive the hard times.

Don't despair just because every day of your marriage does not live up to some romantic dream, the sort that is staged at considerable expense by advertising photographers or invented by workaday novelists for a little light entertainment. It's hard work to make a marriage grow, especially if you are isolated from family and friends who can help and support. It's too easy to think there's something wrong with yourself (or *her*, or *him*) when the promised ecstasy doesn't happen. Romantic fantasy is not a guide to the reality of Christian marriage.

You just can't tell what the future will hold; you cannot be certain that everything will be rosy ever after; and you'd be daft to expect your partner to stay exactly as they are now. It is perhaps because marriage is such a huge undertaking, such a step in the dark, such a long-lasting commitment, that many couples still wish to marry in church and ask God to be part of their life together. God represents a kind of authority and permanence that will provide a solid foundation for the marriage. And that is true—but not as a kind of magic or good-luck charm: rather because through the person of Jesus and through the Bible God shows us how to live in a way that nurtures love and builds relationships.

☆ *Keep talking.* Maybe it seems that right now you never have enough time to talk. But when you live with someone, over the years conversation can dry up or become superficial and empty.

Always take time to talk, and to talk about things that matter. And listen. Never be so busy that you can't give five or ten minutes in the day just to chat and listen, especially when things are strained.

☆ *Don't be afraid to say again and again 'I'm sorry' and 'I love you'.* But try not to say them only in that order. And when you discover in your partner a new talent or strength, or in some way or another are reminded of how special a person they are, tell them!

Praise and encouragement are food and drink to our inner selves. Love that grows is unselfish and looks for ways to build up the other person.

☆ *Be ready to forgive.* So he forgot the anniversary date. She didn't listen on the day he didn't get the promotion. Trivial incidents that stick like barbs, as well as worse calamities, quickly take the shine off romance. It isn't easy to be forgiving.

But we can all call to mind things we have done that would make us blush and yet we know that we still want people to love us. And, however great the fault, God is willing and able to forgive us and go on loving us, the slate wiped clean. For this reason, Christian marriage is about forgiving and not keeping a record of the wrongs done.

That's why your wedding vows are so important. That's why the terribly traditional, easy-to-laugh-at, do-they-still-say-that 'till death us do part' phrase is, in fact, a wonderful declaration of intent. A declaration that the love which God has given you is not intended to wear out prematurely. It's a love which gives you both the security to make mistakes *and* to make up afterwards. It's a love which, in public and in private, is inviting you to reflect through your marriage the love of God—constant, unchanging, faithful.

To be married in church *could* be simply a religious veneer, a silly joke to please the grandparents and to guarantee you a wedding album with all the right photographs. That's what it could be . . .

But it could also be something else: the awakening of a new quality of life. That's when you discover that not only are you loved by your partner, which is no small miracle in itself, but that you are also known and loved, intimately, by the God who made you. To discover that such divine love is the very foundation of your own human love is to begin to discover the truth of what Jesus once said: 'I have come that you might have life; life in all its fullness.'